NG SPACE

Uranus

by Colleen Sexton

Consultant:
Duane Quam, M.S. Physics
Chair, Minnesota State
Academic Science Standards
Writing Committee

BELLWETHER MEDIA • MINNEAPOLIS, MN

Note to Librarians, Teachers, and Parents:

Blastoff! Readers are carefully developed by literacy experts and combine standards-based content with developmentally appropriate text.

Level 1 provides the most support through repetition of high-frequency words, light text, predictable sentence patterns, and strong visual support.

Level 2 offers early readers a bit more challenge through varied simple sentences, increased text load, and less repetition of high-frequency words.

Level 3 advances early-fluent readers toward fluency through increased text and concept load, less reliance on visuals, longer sentences, and more literary language.

Level 4 builds reading stamina by providing more text per page, increased use of punctuation, greater variation in sentence patterns, and increasingly challenging vocabulary.

Level 5 encourages children to move from "learning to read" to "reading to learn" by providing even more text, varied writing styles, and less familiar topics.

Whichever book is right for your reader, Blastoff! Readers are the perfect books to build confidence and encourage a love of reading that will last a lifetime!

This edition first published in 2010 by Bellwether Media, Inc.

Library of Congress Cataloging-in-Publication Data

Sexton, Colleen A., 1967-
Uranus / by Colleen Sexton.
    p. cm. – (Blastoff! readers. exploring space)
Includes bibliographical references and index.
Summary: "Introductory text and full-color images explore the physical characteristics and discovery of the planet Uranus. Intended for students in kindergarten through third grade"–Provided by publisher.
ISBN 978-1-60014-408-0 (hardcover : alk. paper)
1. Uranus (Planet)–Juvenile literature. I. Title.
QB681.S49 2010
523.47–dc22   2009037991

Text copyright © 2010 by Bellwether Media, Inc.
Printed in the United States of America, North Mankato, MN.
010110   1149

Contents

What Is Uranus? 4

Uranus in the Solar System 6

How Uranus Looks 14

Moons and Rings 16

Exploring Uranus 20

Glossary 22

To Learn More 23

Index 24

Uranus is a **planet**. From
Earth it looks like a tiny point
of blue light. For a long time,
people thought it was a **star**.

Astronomer

William Herschel used a **telescope** to study the blue light in 1781. He discovered that it was a planet.

William Herschel

Uranus is part of the **solar system**. All of the planets in the solar system **orbit** the sun.

Uranus

Uranus is the seventh planet from the sun. It is about 1.8 billion miles (2.9 billion kilometers) away.

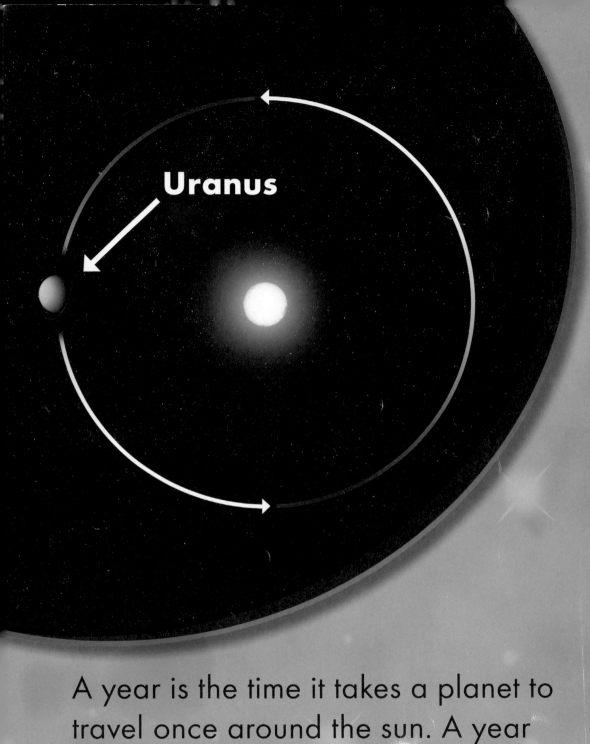

Uranus

A year is the time it takes a planet to travel once around the sun. A year on Uranus equals 84 Earth years.

A day is the time it takes a planet to spin around once. A day on Uranus equals about 17 Earth hours.

axis

Uranus spins on an imaginary line through its center called an **axis**. Most planets have a vertical axis.

Uranus' axis runs from side to side. Scientists think a large space object hit Uranus and knocked it on its side.

Earth

Uranus

Uranus is the third largest
planet. It is 31,764 miles (51,118
kilometers) wide. About 63 Earths
could fit inside Uranus.

Little of the sun's heat reaches Uranus. It is a cold planet. The temperature of the **atmosphere** is about −357° Fahrenheit (−216° Celsius).

Uranus does not have a solid surface. It is made of gases and liquids. A gas called **methane** gives Uranus its blue-green color.

Strong winds blow clouds on Uranus into long bands. These bands make Uranus look striped.

Oberon

Umbriel

Miranda

Ariel

Uranus has 27 **moons**.
The five largest moons are
Ariel, Miranda, Titania,
Oberon, and Umbriel.

Titania

Miranda is famous for the deep **grooves** on its surface. They look like frosting swirls on a cake.

grooves

At least 13 thin **rings** circle Uranus. They are made of rocks and dust.

← **rings**

The rings are hard to see. Astronomers did not find them until almost 200 years after the discovery of Uranus.

Most knowledge about Uranus came from *Voyager 2*. This **space probe** flew by the planet in 1986.

Voyager 2

telescope

Astronomers will
study Uranus with
new telescopes.
They want to learn
more about this
sideways planet.

Glossary

astronomer—a scientist who studies space and objects in space

atmosphere—the gases around an object in space

axis—an imaginary line that runs through the center of a planet; a planet spins on its axis.

grooves—long, narrow cuts in a surface

methane—a gas in Uranus's atmosphere; methane gives Uranus its blue-green color.

moons—space objects that orbit a planet or other space object

orbit—to travel around the sun or other object in space

planet—a large, round space object that orbits the sun and is alone in its orbit

rings—flat bands made of rock, dust, and ice around a planet; rings look solid from far away.

solar system—the sun and the objects that orbit it; the solar system has planets, moons, comets, and asteroids.

space probe—a spacecraft that explores planets and other space objects and sends information back to Earth; space probes do not carry people.

star—a large ball of burning gases in space

telescope—a tool that makes faraway objects look larger and nearer

To Learn More

AT THE LIBRARY

Howard, Fran. *Uranus*. Edina, Minn.: ABDO Publishing, 2008.

Slade, Suzanne. *A Look at Uranus*. New York, N.Y.: PowerKids Press, 2008.

Taylor-Butler, Christine. *Uranus*. New York, N.Y.: Children's Press, 2005.

ON THE WEB

Learning more about Uranus is as easy as 1, 2, 3.

1. Go to www.factsurfer.com.

2. Enter "Uranus" into the search box.

3. Click the "Surf" button and you will see a list of related Web sites.

With factsurfer.com, finding more information is just a click away.

BLASTOFF! JIMMY CHALLENGE

Blastoff! Jimmy is hidden somewhere in this book. Can you find him? If you need help, you can find a hint at the bottom of page 24.

Index

1781, 5
1986, 20
Ariel, 16
astronomer, 5, 19, 21
atmosphere, 13
axis, 10, 11
clouds, 15
color, 4, 5, 14
day, 9
Earth, 4, 12
gases, 14
grooves, 17
Herschel, William, 5
liquids, 14
methane, 14
Miranda, 16, 17
moons, 16
Oberon, 16
orbit, 6
planet, 4, 5, 6, 7, 8, 9,
    10, 12, 13, 20, 21
rings, 18, 19

scientists, 11
solar system, 6
space probe, 20
star, 4
sun, 6, 7, 8, 13
surface, 14, 17
telescope, 5, 21
temperature, 13
Titania, 16, 17
Umbriel, 16
Voyager 2, 20
winds, 15
year, 8

The images in this book are reproduced through the courtesy of: Juan Martinez, front cover, pp. 8, 9, 10, 12, 14-15, Mark Garlick / Alamy, p. 4; The Print Collector, p. 5 (small); NASA, pp. 6 7, 11, 16 17, 17 (small), 20-21; Julian Baum / Science Photo Library, p. 13; Mark Garlick / Science Photo Library, pp. 18 (small), 18-19.

Blastoff! Jimmy Challenge (from page 23).
Hint: Go to page 15 and it will come to you out of the blue.